Celebrating the Peoples and Civilizations of Southeast Asia™

THE HMONG

Dolly Brittan

The Rosen Publishing Group's
PowerKids Press™
New York

Published in 1997 by The Rosen Publishing Group, Inc.
29 East 21st Street, New York, NY 10010

First Edition

Book Design: Danielle Primiceri

Photo Credits: Cover © J. P. Valentín/ANAKO Editions (background); Juan Sabourdy/ANAKO Editions (front); p. 4 © C. Michel/ANAKO Editions; pp. 7, 8, 16, 19 (top, middle) © J. P. Valentín/ANAKO Editions; pp. 11, 19 (background) M. Huteau/ANAKO Editions; pp. 12, 15 © Patrick Bernard/ANAKO Editions; p. 19 (bottom) © Xiaomin Feng/ANAKO Editions.

Brittan, Dolly.
    The Hmong / Dolly Brittan.
        p.   cm. (Celebrating the peoples and civilizations of Southeast Asia)
    ISBN 0-8239-5128-6
    1. Hmong (Asian people)—Juvenile literature. I. Title. II. Series.
    DS570.M5B75 1996
    305.895'942—dc21   97-10184
                                                                                 CIP
                                                                                 AC

Manufactured in the United States of America

Contents

The Hmong People

The **Hmong** (huh-MONG) people are made up of many smaller groups of people. The Hmong live in Asia and Southeast Asia, in countries such as China, Thailand, Vietnam, and Laos. Some Hmong live in America, France, and Australia. In China, the Hmong are usually called the **Miao** (mee-OW).

The name Hmong in the Hmong language means "free people." In order to keep their freedom, many Hmong have had to move from their homeland in the mountains of China.

The mountains of China were once home to the Hmong. Today, the Hmong live all over the world.

The History of the Hmong

It is believed that the Hmong **culture** (KUL-cher) began in the Hunan Province in what is now the country of China. Records show that the Hmong culture goes back to 618 A.D. But many people believe the Hmong culture has been around for thousands of years. When the Chinese began to rule over the Hmong in the 1800s, many Hmong left China. They moved to countries in Southeast Asia, such as Laos and Thailand. Millions of Hmong now live in other parts of the world. About 5 million Hmong are still in China.

The Hmong culture is very old. An important part of this culture is the colorful clothing that many Hmong women make. ▶

What Is Hmong Culture?

It is hard to say exactly what Hmong culture is. Many Hmong, such as those living in Laos and Thailand, have kept Hmong **customs** (KUS-tumz) while learning the customs of the country they now live in. Other Hmong, such as those in China, still follow many of the **traditional** (truh-DISH-un-ul) Hmong customs. Still other Hmong, such as those in the United States, may no longer practice Hmong customs. However, there are some basic beliefs and customs that are the same for Hmong all over the world.

◄ *It is a tradition among the Hmong in China to dress up in clothes decorated with silver for festivals.*

Ways of Life

Many Hmong live in the mountains of their chosen countries. Some are farmers. They raise crops, such as corn, potatoes, peanuts, and sugarcane. It is believed that many of these Hmong move every ten years to a new village and fresh, new land on which to farm. Other Hmong choose to live on the coast or at the foothills of the mountains. Some work in big cities. Others have rice farms. On these farms, rice is planted in fields, called paddies, that are flooded with water. Some farmers raise fish in the flooded rice paddies.

Many Hmong are farmers who grow rice. ▶

The Language

The Hmong language has many **dialects** (DY-uh-lekts). The written Hmong language was lost long ago. The Chinese did not allow people to read or write Hmong. Some Hmong women tried to save the alphabet by stitching the letters onto their clothes. Some of the letters were saved, but no one knows what these letters mean.

A new written language was created about 50 years ago. Today, many Hmong are able to read and write in Hmong, as well as the language of the country in which they live.

◄ *Today, many Hmong children learn to speak, read, and write their language in school.*

Religion

Many of the Hmong who live in China and Southeast Asia follow religious beliefs called **animism** (AN-im-izm). Animism is the belief that all living things have spirits. **Shamans** (SHAH-menz) are also very important in Hmong culture. They are spiritual leaders who help guide people through hard times, illness, and important events. Many Hmong also practice **ancestor worship** (AN-ses-ter WER-ship). This is when a family shows great respect for members who lived before, such as grand-parents and great-grandparents.

Animists believe that spirits live in all things, including animals. ▶

Music and Singing

Music and singing are very important to the Hmong. The **khene** (KEN-eh), or bamboo flute, has been used by the Hmong for over 2,000 years. Most *khene* can be held in a person's hand. But some are so large they must be held by two people or be played while they sit on the ground. A large *khene* can be heard for miles. The *khene* was once used to call warriors to fight. Now it is used for ceremonies. Singing is another large part of Hmong culture. Many Hmong sing to each other every day to tell each other special things, such as "I love you."

There is a special area in many villages that is set aside just for playing the khene. *Men play the* khene *and other instruments during festivals.*

Colorful Clothing

It is a tradition for Hmong women to wear bright, colorful clothing. These clothes are often decorated with beautiful **embroidery** (em-BROY-der-ee). Hmong girls learn to embroider when they are about five years old. It takes years to become very good at embroidering. The women sew many patterns, including dragons, tigers, lions, and flowers. The patterns change depending on where the person lives. Some patterns tell whole stories.

Hmong women must first make the cloth before they can embroider their beautiful designs on it. ▶

Food

Because it is hard for the Hmong who live in the mountains to get to markets, they learned to **preserve** (pre-ZERV) their food. They preserve vegetables, such as peppers, eggplant, cucumbers, and beans, by adding salt and storing them in jars. This pickles the food and makes it last for a long time. The Hmong preserve meats, such as chicken and duck, by smoking it over a fire.

The Hmong eat rice with nearly every meal.

◀ *It can be hard to find fresh food among the Hmong villages in the mountains. The people there must prepare food so it will last for a long time.*

Keeping the Culture

Because the Hmong live in so many countries, speak so many languages, and have lost many Hmong customs, many people fear that they will lose their culture. In order for the Hmong culture to **survive** (ser-VYV), it is important that Hmong children learn about their culture and take pride in it.

Many Hmong women have embroidered blankets and quilts with traditional Hmong designs and stories. These blankets and quilts are then sold to people all over the world. This is one way to pass on Hmong history. In this way, the Hmong culture will survive and grow.

Glossary

ancestor worship (AN-ses-ter WER-ship) To respect the family members that lived before you.

animism (AN-im-izm) The belief that all living things have spirits.

culture (KUL-cher) The beliefs and customs of a group of people.

custom (KUS-tum) The accepted, respected way of doing something.

dialect (DY-uh-lekt) A form of a language that is spoken by a certain group of people.

embroidery (em-BROY-der-ee) Designs sewn into cloth with a needle.

Hmong (huh-MONG) A group of people who came from Asia, and are now scattered throughout the world. Also the name for the traditional language of the Hmong people.

khene (KEN-eh) The Hmong name for their traditional bamboo flute.

Miao (mee-OW) The Chinese name for the Hmong.

preserve (pre-ZERV) To keep from spoiling.

shaman (SHAH-men) A spiritual leader who helps guide people through hard times, illness, and important events.

survive (ser-VYV) To keep alive.

traditional (truh-DISH-un-ul) A way of doing something that is passed down from parent to child.

23

Index